POEMS
FOR EVER

POEMS
FOR EVER

KUMAR BOSE

ZORBA BOOKS

ZB

ZORBA BOOKS

Publishing Services in India by Zorba Books, 2018

Website: www.zorbabooks.com
Email: info@zorbabooks.com

Copyright © Kumar Bose

ISBN 978-93-88497-14-5
E-Book:-978-93-88497-15-2

Zorba Books Pvt. Ltd.(opc)
Gurgaon, INDIA

CONTENTS

PREFACE

KUMAR BOSE

This is a collection of my virtual poems – the real ones are buried in me. The human mind is designed or even used to retaining a little within, not for sharing, and this is precisely the disability. Thoughts do not come in rhymes.

From a very early age I've grown with keen senses, compassion being its cornerstone. So, my poems tend to be biased – one may say one sided or even asymmetrically poised. My humble upbringing infused in me a will to look at life on a frameless canvas – ever extendable, emancipated - free from set notions and verses. At no point of my journey have I forgotten that I'm a cosmic being – rotating, revolving and sliding at a god sent speed to the Great Attractor. We all are co-passengers.

I'm a late starter in my endeavour, having had to devote the most part of my energy and thoughts in stale routine for a worldly living. It's only in last few years that my key board has gone poetic, so to say.

I look forward keenly to remaining in communication with the readers, who may like to assume for themselves the role of an editor-by- choice, for enhancing the poesy.

For I know, there is a poet hidden in every reader of poetry.

Kumar Bose
KOLKATA
mail : bosetk20@gmail.com   20th September,2018.

Desire

Where cosmic silence resonates with new born stars,
where time sleeps through eternity,
where extant souls

stream across galaxies in vain;
somewhere there,   5
divine aurora caresses
slopes of her pensive face -
longing for life.
Her frozen tears
emitting desire on eyelashes -   10
ushered into icicles on fir leaves
under a drowsy terrestrial sun;
she is ever dying to be reborn here -
on this alluring earth.

Vision

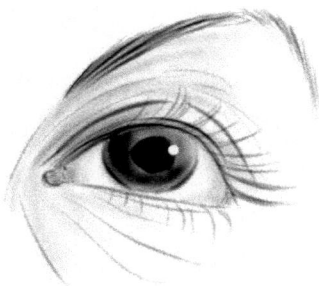

A skyful of stardust,
wading through a sea of frozen darkness,
filled my eyes
with fluorescent waves
of colours and shades -   5
erupting in a spring of delight.

My vision bloomed
in surging trance,
into a sparkling stream of images,
across near, far and beyond –   10
freeing my captive senses
from the agony of bondage.

My tears of joy and sorrow
often wash these images-
stuck in my eyes for years,   15
turning bright and luminous,
awaking blurry memories.

Often, they spill out of my eyes
in bubbles of glossy reminiscences -
floating away in the aimless breeze of time;   20
then, the flutter of rain-soaked leaves
on a gusty monsoon night,
or rustling fall leaves
booting an autumn siesta,
bring back a few drifting bubbles   25
from the threshold of obscurity.

Now, since twilight is settling in layers
to relieve a tired sun,
to drown the firmament into darkness,
I'm waiting to release these images   30
into the infinite
I borrowed from.

Virtual Poem

A poem is the mirror image
of bubbles adrift in mind;
thoughts real, poems virtual–
meddled, dilute and unkind.

One brews in the poet's mind,   5
the other to blend as poesy;
thoughts melt–humbled on the way,
in fervour, pain or glee.

Poem is the mind's child
born of swarming bees,   10
churned out in moments-
joyous, painful and pensive.
Or born of a violent surge
from the eye of a storm,
blown off to a strange verge-   15
often lost, often stillborn.

So am I to my poem-
an echo sans script,
that livens up a vacuum,
as the mind takes wing   20
over the horizon lay near,
or into the sky afar,
riding the animated earth-
spinning and skirting;
afloat the eyes on street,   25
amidst the real world I abhor,
or the unreal I crave for,
or the fake ones I'm beset with.

Often thoughts reach me,
buoyed by trade winds;   30
or abstract ones
feeble to precipitate,
or play hide and seek
in the dark alleys of mind-
groping for the sun;   35
Or the ones that whisper
day and night,
in sorrow and delight.

Virtual poem, what I can offer-
dusting bits of cut and paste: 40
shapely, flowing, ornate;
provoke twice, once be fake,
that brings in its wake
labour pain of creation.

Virtual poems to breathe here,   45
the real ones, buried in me.

Mariana Trench

Behold the planet in blue!
It's flat and round,
it's dark and bright,
it's plain at places,
also, at a dizzy height.   5

It revolves and spins,
it's moving, yet still;
it spans the blue sky above,
tucks the sky below as a frill.
It draws the power of the sun,   10
to keep us fed and bright;
it bathes baby-moon,
in soft, faint-glow light.
It's balmy in foliage,
glaring on arid sand;   15
it's furious in Vesuvius,
Fuji, Kilimanjaro, so grand.
She's the mother earth,
source of all our being;
we write poems on her,   20
make merry and sing.

She isn't keeping well - of late,
she's sick and frail,
what's more - she's hurt
and angry in her veil,   25
for what we've done to her,
to the air, water and soil;
we've toyed with all she gave,
like a wayward child!

Her trip-time slowing,   30
lungs breathing toxin,
her glaciers melting bare,
species being extinct;
her oceans swallowing heritage land,
habitats under frequent fury,   35
stubborn wastes filling her belly,
porous, is her protective canopy.
Beyond we go to junk her space-
to imprint a sullen human face.

Often do I get terrifying dream-   40
that, trees nowhere to be seen;
not a speck of cloud in the air,
snow-lines lay bare;
Earth, oceans - scorched and thirsty,
all its vapour escaped gravity.   45
I'm in Guam, by empty Pacific-
trying to fathom the gorge of
deep, dark hazed Mariana Trench.

———————◦◉◦◦———————

Today

I love my Today,
born of the mighty Sun
in the cradle of the Earth.
Can touch and feel it bare,
hear its psalm - loud and clear;   5
bear its indulgence – here and there,
yet remain rapt in it
till it slips and melts into
the dark grains of the night-
into Yesterday.   10

My ephemeral Today- not keen
to incarnate as Tomorrow;
nor to eavesdrop
the moaning of the anterior day,
that got buried   15
under the heaves of
dead moments
only the prior night.

My Today is ever moist-
a floret, opening face at dawn,   20
catching eyes of the butterflies;
swinging between mosaic of dates-
fallen lifeless or kindling hopes,
in the pages of an eternal calendar.

Ecstasy overwhelms!   25
My Todays seen decomposed
into ruins and tombs
to the delight of archaeologists,
toiling to excavate slain Todays
and missing the most-   30
not spared a space
in the memory of bygone time.

Who is keen
on an enigmatic Tomorrow
at Today's cost!   35
Life perishes stealthily
before Tomorrow sets in.
It's all Today, but Today!
Tomorrow waits for it-
like an heir apparent   40
marking time for the crown.

I need to clear
my cupboards of all skeletons;
I want more space for my Today.

Seeing
It Many Ways

Reality - a mere illusion:
said a great thinker.
Brain – not eyes, has the final say,
perception though may tinker.
Illusory checks help us navigate,   5
other times may trick us:
everything we come across,
a figment of imagination – ignis fatuus.

Child sees through magical eyes,
the world that floats around;   10
sense to soon dawn with the sun,
to initiate him to play and fun.

A mundane soul sees what eyes meet,
his wiser self is more discreet;
he sees back and forth to act,   15
squeezes all he sees to fact.

A visually impaired 'sees' through senses-
of touch, taste, hearing or smell;
light for him a synonym of darkness,
all he sees is built through tales.   20
A hearing impaired sees silent time
tick by - through touch, taste or smell;
frozen silence surrounds forever,
glass would break to rhythm, if it fell.

When mind is sunk in trailing thoughts,   25
fear, jitter, awe – creep and grope;
vision blurs to shut the eyes,
all he sees - what truth belies.

Blinded by love, hate, greed or anger,
when emotions rein on – impulse stronger;   30
his vision reaches where whim dictates,
best his haste makes mindless wastes.

Where foresight saves, eyes may rue,
what we see may reduce to optics;
'Seeing is believing'– struggles to live on,   35
video can't be the arbiter of justice.

When pretence is the name of the game,
played to deceive a naive grace;
all he relies - on a make belief
that a gossamer veil can hide a face.   40

Distance vision seeks to bridge
where eyes aren't meant to reach,
probing minds have grasps so strong
that imagery and entity make a bond.

Cosmonauts zoom into mesmeric space   45
amidst heaven unfolding around,
mind yet hovers around the blue globe
when eclipsed in orbit behind the moon.

Hope, fantasy, nightmare,
sub-conscious desire and wish-   50
stored in images to make a dream:
non-real setting –of no consequence!

When born with sight impaired,
never perceived an image or a gleam;
other sensory strings act on,   55
recalling memory in auditory dream.

Strange enough we refuse to see,
climate change is out to lay
all species that roam the earth:
must Man commit this felo-de-se!   60

Epitaph

Craggy walls and tyrannic bars,
Dingy, ghoulish, dank shelters;
Flogging dungeon, servile labour,
Dreadful dream and hay fever;
I bore the brunt of time.
My violent heart
Would moan not a word,
I walked past the gallows to the past;
I perished for a cause divine.

Rag Picker

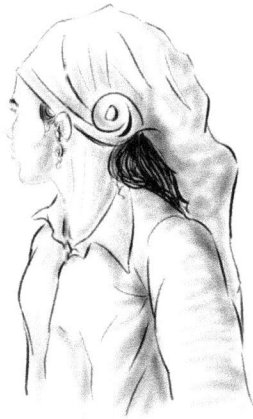

Dawn has barely taken
the lid off the city's filth,
she's back on her slight frame
for yet another grinding time;
rag-shack hung from her shoulder,   5
a shrunken child left behind
in a shanty cluster
edging a sewage-channel,
at the fringe of a scornful city.

She raises qualm and hatred 10
from criss-crossing early risers,
who would walk a mile or two
to burn their cuddled fat.
Street dogs bark at her oddity-
of a species outlandish, 15
trying to push her beyond the city limits
with pique and peeve.

She's a rag picker- the vibes
of my anaemic poem;
a single mother 20
who collects city wastes,
a stranger to the mayor,
worry of the police and
eye sore of the community.
She's resigned to much more, 25
having lost her soul
in the rub of life.

She rushes through her picks,
digging up with hands and feet,
for a hefty harvest of sorts: 30
plastics and packages
clean or filthy, black or brown,
cans and bottles, often leery ones,
scraps - fresh or stenchy,
sharp and piercing. 35

A lot of pick is her need,
away she had stayed
the whole week-
nursing the baby in endemic.
Good luck springs from a heap-   40
a welcome pack intact,
a leftover from the night's feast;
last she ate a day before,
the handler hadn't cleared her score.

Entangled in stress and distress,   45
she has stopped looking for an escape.
Has no nation to her entity,
no social space to hole up-
a persona non grata on own soil;
yet, she is a cog in 'Clean India' wheel.   50
The city draws a free service,
her sufferings notwithstanding.

She coughs her way
through lanes and dumps,
her feet tire and move,   55
in tandem with day and night;
she picks the scraps of borrowed time,
carrying 'Swachh Bharat' in her sack.

Leaves and Buds

Somewhere rests a lush green bowl
in clover of an azure hill, canvassing
white, puffy, caressing clouds,
and purling of spa-guzzling brooks;
passing showers swing across the field,   5
bringing cool message from uphill.
The night sky stares at the dusky field
in the stillness of mischievous mist.
I reached thus - your bushy hamlet of bliss.

Rain drops set you in the rhythm of life,   10
birds sing on and on from the shade trees -
'Pothey kootoom', 'pothey kootoom'
(the guest is on the way) -
blending a rhapsody the whole night,
and you lay blissfully on your leafy bed.   15

Mellowed sun shows up from a showery night,
with a thousand gleeful sparkles
peeping through the breezy leaves of Albizias -
drawing you from a monsoon trance.

Rainy nights follow bright days,   20
and soon you leap into your teens,
gathering all the flavour and vigour,
that discerning eyes miss never.

Caring fingers pick you one day
from your homestead,   25
ushering into a world wider,
to groom you for the finale.
You fill the air with innate aroma,
as you're dressed in the makeover,
with a deft touch of your mentor.   30

You walk the ramp with grace and fervour,
and adorn the podium in catchy outfits -
to win the limits of land and race;
become the epitome of tradition and culture,
stimulating thoughts and bonding minds.   35

I salute thee,
the soulful
'One bud and two leaves' -
my adorable cup of Tea.
Yes, the guests would soon be here,   40
to share the gift of your essence.

Soul Mind and Me

The immortal, immaterial being in me,
the emotional, intellectual element in me,
O' my soul! When did you sneak into my cage-
to make its spiritual core,
to infuse a meaning into me.   5
Elusive, as always you are
in your shadowless, spirited obscurity;
while you choose to remain alien to me,
I'm glued between mind and temporal entity.

Yes, mind is my inseparable company, day and night,   10
evoking desire, volition, thoughts and feelings;
shaping memory, conscience and opinion,
focus, attitude and attention;
and must it evaporate
as I leave this worldly abode!   15
There, in the labyrinth,
mind is eternally craving
for an answer from the soul,
if it would ever give up its nomadic self,
of hopping life to life – incognito,   20
from here to eternity.

Looking for Heaven

Presume for once, there is a heaven
somewhere deep in the cosmos,
where gods reside in peace for ever,
remote-sense their creations' cause.

Heaven, world of its own,   5
encased in a nebular haze,
obscured from a distance gaze,
forbidden to mortal access.

Nothing perishes, no one dies,
time is frozen, day never cries;   10
seasons at will - rain or spring,
idioms of god, birds sing.
Petals of colours sky showers,
sprinkles stardust in fairy nights,
wind blows sweet fragrance,   15
fountains dance with springy sprights.

Extinct species roam the arcadia,
gods have saved them to live;
fruits and flowers fill Eden,
buzzing bees store nectar in hives.   20

Dreamy glows in their wings
fairies raise ripples on harp,
rain crystals shimmer in the sky,
dawn and dusk descend in hymns.
Divine Assembly meets as often   25
as the mortals dip in sins;
sect, faith, colour all bloom here,
ubiquitous gods, now here now there.

I do not have count of the gods,
my guess would be as good as yours;   30
need to first sum up the planets,
and tally faiths tagged thereof.

Craving for heaven-an enigma,
fables of reaching heaven-a myth,
preaching insular scripts-a ploy,   35
Shangri-La is here for us to bequeath.

Dubai

A humble overture made
to the ridiculing falcons glide by:
'Come down to Mother Earth and see,
a wingless flier soaring into your sky'!

Archaic is the sky through the ages,   5
as we see its reign from the earth;
Dubai aesthetics stacked in its yard,
like supertalls composed on blue pages.

Drawing near the sky to pluck
all the jewels - so studded,   10
to indulge in its eternal lust,
for gems and gold - so lauded!

Majestic condos in curved tops,
sparkling crests that dotted the skyline;
they rise from the Creek with first light,   15
afloat in sleepy eyes the whole night.

Jaw-dropping beauties—bright and smiley,
veiled ones adorn the haze of the Milky Way;
come, see and hold emotions
on the'banks' of the Business Bay.   20

Shopaholics' beeline to glitzy malls,
escapades to sand dunes - so exotic;
'A thousand and one nights' comes alive,
the cascading garden weaves an aqua magic.

Rugged heights overlooking sand dunes,   25
pristine beaches and lush green parks;
vintage Arab flavour being redefined in-
Palm Jumeirah, Hydropolis or Twisting Towers.

Human grit seeks to raise
an Arab dream onto the sky;   30
they all flock around this 'City of Gold'-
for a glimpse of mystique Dubai.

Sigh

A gush of C O two pumped into the air,
emptying lungs - slow or fast,
that seldom has words to precede or follow,
that sets the mind, relieved or hollow;
it's a sigh - of a state of mind,   5
of emotions, all kinds.

A long deep breath
audibly emitted,
to express in their own ways-
sadness or weariness,   10
longing or relief,
anxiety or disbelief.

When the wait for a loved one is long,
when in mind a loss drags on,
remembered childhood,   15
or a yearn for parenthood;
when heaves of "ifs" gather
hope bubbles or new feathers,
even as the hair goes grey or falls,
or stare in vain at moment's calls.   20

On being replied 'no' or 'never',
'That's all' or 'it's over'!
sigh – sigh and sigh
for one and all – low or high.

All by itself and very own,   25
no anger, joy or despair shown;
lone sound that mind only speaks,
has no colour - land or creed.

Sigh that follows on threading a needle,   30
naïve to have a veiled meaning,
but sigh be aware may spill a bin,
he who sighs but holds the bearing.

Can you hear the muted sigh-
that of a solitary tomb,   35
or that rises from a wayward stream-
round pebbles strewn around.
When rain-drops first soaked in years,
sigh of relief shall then you hear.

Sigh of sadness demands to be felt,   40
sigh of distress deserves to be dealt;
but sigh as a trait needs to be shed,
to separate the real from the fake.

Heavy wind sighs through the trees-
into the valley of dry pine;   45
the Poet but sighs reclined in a couch,
laments the lack of rain and shine.

Reticence

O darling! You asked me
how I fancied you - I portrayed you.
Could there be a loftier task
than to draw you
in tossed off, futile words!   5

In quandary,
my lips were unmoved,
reticence held my speech,
voice choked
in a puff of wows,   10
mind trod in the labyrinth
in quest of a divine motif,
for an eternal portrait.

1945

On a day - early autumn,
mid-forties, twentieth century,
the world by then had learnt to live
with macabre of the raging war.

Piercing blasts of shells and human cries -   5
risen from the venomous blitzkrieg,
still spewing stench and fear into the skies;
canines and prey birds extending a feast
on heaved up human carcasses
of soldiers, women, children and the frails.   10
Yelling dogs and wolves renting the night skies –
spreading message of horror, now and then;
numb, shadowy, drifting prisoners,
still crowding death cells in eerie camps -
like swarms of earthworm   15
beset with mass graves;
groans of live sex dolls pitching
to escape desolate billet rows.

Settling scores are rival armies in beastly ferocity.
Wrecks of planes and vessels lay scattered   20
amid ruins of runways, ports, railroads;
many more gathering moss on deep, dark ocean-beds.
Blown off roofs, ruined living blocks, pounded bridges
lay strewn in camps, neighbourhoods and cities.
The heavy fall of boots, armoured carriers and war
planes   25
now and then tearing through the pitch-dark
silence of night.
Hustling nations still joining the fray for a share
of the pie,
while crippled ones yet to pick up the threads
of sense and sensibilities.

Gasping still, nuke-hit ground-zeroes with aftershocks. 30
Flattened homes, blown-off in a wink of eye;
Human: with melted flesh, kinked and singed hair
hung down from the temple over cheek,
dangling over the mouth,
eye lids drawn up,eyes burned out   35
leaving black holes instead,
still roam the ruins of roasted cities
over flash-burnt mortals lay in silence,
as death stalks countless victims
of burns, shock and radiation sickness.   40

Reprisal and revenge being taken
on retreating armies and prisoners -
amidst cities being raged all over;
freedom being timed here and there;
glitzy admirals, SS men opting ritual suicide   45
for failing to defend or for reprieve.
Occupation Armies looting villages all the way,
leaving scorched earth behind.

One such day of September, 1945
the darkest year ever- 50
when I entered the world
amidst inflamed history erupting all around.
If I were born for a passage
through a sane new world,
or with scripted holocausts 55
revisiting the earth!
The year wanted an answer.

Monologue

Childhood!
Why do you walk alongside,
clasping my finger now and then
with your tender fist,
asking from your creamy lips,   5
in so many inchoate words,
recount of bygone days;
haven't we parted decades ago!

Why do you look into my eyes
walking down memory lane,   10
criss-crossing alleys of time,
hearing from your loved ones
chides in shadowy voice,
and you try to undo,
with a look of guilt-   15
all that is not to their taste.

Why do you run up
to a torrent stream
to swim across,
and scare me of an inane mess.   20
why do you glance back
as I follow your boyish steps,
through the heat and dust
of a summer noon-
reaching for ripe mangoes   25
on swaying tree tops
of a desolate orchard;
Its fearsome loneliness
up there, haunts me still.

The ill lit pages of your books   30
under the flickering flame of an oil lamp,
working hard to hold its breath
against a gusty distressing wind;
I can barely see
through the haze of time,   35
your sleepy eyes
weaving cobweb of early lessons.

Memories of Holi splashes,
or of flying sparkles of lights
in festive Diwali nights,   40
or of a long Puja carnival
spent in juvenile freedom,
often leave me breathless
with bubbly joy and longing.

Yes, I hear your prompting-   45
of frolics in school picnics,
of cycling down the high road
throwing all cautions to the wind,
of suffering in days of illness,
with the mother wading through   50
wakeful nights by your bed side.

And not to shy away
from the latent love,
you treasured
for the Lady Teacher who   55
held the class riveted.

Pebbles of colours and shapes
were many to pick,
on the shores of memory deep.
I can barely relive 60
having lost you
in the din of adolescence.

How I long to be with you,
turning the wheel of time!
Grow with you once more, 65
to leave foot-prints along
the unbeaten star-lit path,
to round up a life that's worth.

To the Bird

Take me on your wings
to endless freedom,
to the starry sky
into galactic dreams,
to the crescent   5
kissing the amorous earth
in the wee hours of night,
to the fluorescence of first light
erasing gloom on its flight,
to the rainbow-   10
into the shower of cosmic colours,
to the fantasy of weightless journey
from vales to hills,
into the lull of a brewing storm-
to playfully flutter back   15
to the canopy of a rain forest.

Take me on your wings,
to break away from human stories-
soaked in blood and tears;
take me on your wings   20
to share your endless joy-
your moments of ipseity.

Take me on your wings again,
for your tweets and songs;
how I long to hear its symphony,   25
lost in the din
of the chaotic rumble of life.

Take me on your wings once more
to the heights of the Himalayas,
to raise the sleeping Buddha   30
for his blessing,
on the path to Nirvana.

Of Bondage, Liberty and Freedom

Freedom seeks no definition:
to define is to confine.

Birds, the freest of the living world,
sure, not aware of it!
they just celebrate the sky: 5
to be aware is to restrict.
Animals roam the woods,
stray beyond their 'own' space,
unaware of the limits of living,
for, hunger knows no grace.   10
Microbes multiply in a world
that knows no hold to divide;
species come and go in nature:
evolution is free for all to compete.

Cuckoos choose spring to sing,   15
sand dunes mingle, to desert at will;
fireflies free to search the marshes,
fragrance rides the wind in style.

Clouds are free to sail and thunder,
water is free to fall and plunder,   20
wind is free to howl and wander,
such is nature - untamed. unaware.

I would rather not own this expanse
of freedom that has no definition,
what prevents is our story   25
of lineage and cerebral distinction.

As opposed to freedom,
the story of bondage is of antiquity -
a carnal practice of high hominoids;
war was natural, peace inimical,   30
a slave meant a property in mortal.

One person owning another,
secured at birth, by sale or capture;
'divine' right of the stronger
to rule over equals- by- birth.   35

Injury to slave was akin to damage,
to assets made of body, not soul;
women, children were preferred bonds,
concubines served lust of the strong.

Colonists shipped live cargo -   40
trading arms, liquor and tobacco;
lying on sides were loaded slaves,
in cargo holds of ships for space.

Male slaves worth an orchard,
slaves owning another as gift;   45
allowed even to raise a family,
for a new crop of slaves to breed.

Early men lacked a word for freedom,
history gave space to kings than slaves;
modelled on the taming of animals,   50
legacy destined to not dissipate.

Euphrates, Niles, Indus or Yangtze,
Black Sea, Amazon, Mississippi or Tennessee -
failed to wash their blood and tears;
Polynesians black-birded into a pacific grave.   55

'Freedom' rose from the ashes of bondage!
Lodestars held true wisdom and torque,
to turn the wheel of consequences
into the dawn of liberty and suffrage.

Liberty falters:
people struggled for secular freedom,   60
got in turn autonomy or sovereignty;
rights and charters are jargons of intent,
redeemers fight new domination stealthy.

Independence, the lofty concept-
a cherished symbol of liberty.   65
Oath of want, will and hope
seldom breaks down to society.

The state of being redeemed and free,
still eludes the world at large;
union of nations seems so content   70
with the semblance of liberty and purge.

Territories held by elite nations
thousand miles from their own;
drawing hybrid political patterns,
to serve interests carefully grown.   75

Non-Self-Governing, Crown dependency,
Independently administrated jurisdiction,
Territorial collectivity, SAR tags,
External or Unincorporated territory,
Self-governing state in free association,   80
Unorganised incorporated territory,
Associated non-independent state;
so much the legacies that still plague.

Independent states too grinding liberty,
in the crucible of apathy and denial;   85
persecution on identities and gender,
fleeing refugees – all broken asunder.

Road to freedom:
compassion and love know no religion,
eternal are free letters and speech;   90
freedom from violence, hunger, ignorance-
be the singular order of the legion.

Remove the hurdles to global freedom:
cubicles of nationhood that fractionate.
Dismantle divisive mental barriers,   95
lower the flags amid the beating of drums.

Diffuse and bury all lethal weapons,
demob all national armies into forces,
that would uphold fair courts,
to instil justice for peace and progress.   100

To the Tree

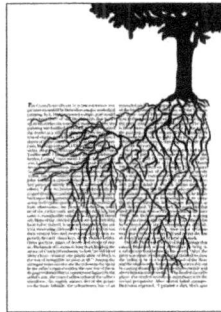

Whose curse befell
that you're moored
in your own turf!
What beset the pith
that you breathe   5
the silence of a tomb!
Who weighed upon
so much vigour
that you give it all
in boundless pity!   10
Why wallow in grief
to a woodland inferno!
why did you baulk
at the will of God,
be the lone living immotile   15
of his creation!

Tranquil ridges and
teeming shores,
mystic forests
or scenic meadows;   20
you meditate for us -
a pastoral habitat.
Bring – elixir of life
to ailing souls,
bouquets of love,   25
and juicy harvests;
breed the homeless -
the flying nomads,
the countless inmates
of an opaque world;   30
keep arid rage
at a distant bay,
shield campers
from sweltering ray.

I hear your hymn,   35
through windy nights,
or, is it the wailing
of your repressed soul!
Do I see you
try to break loose   40
your shackle of woes
in squally time!
Falling a silent prey
to greedy axes,
as lame donees blissfully lay.   45

A parched land at a distance
raises revolt in a sand storm,
tired nomadic dunes
look for a lee of relief,
rain and sand cry foul   50
over the onus of desertion -
echoed in the sands of Kalahari.

Euthanasia

One in vying millions,
chosen to sprout to life;
the will of God springs,
breathes the foetus alive.
It's his wish again   5
to instil soul and mind,
that the child may grow
spirited, creative and kind.

Auspicious, as the child is born,
snapping the days in womb-   10
to roam land, sea and air,
soaked in sun, joy and despair.

Full blown, as the child is grown,
cuts a caper or a niche his own.
Deeds, the world may love or hate,   15
journey through life hinged on fate!

Quite flows the river, so the time,
life may flicker earlier than prime.
Twilight sure shall catch up with age,
as the mortal drifts to low ebb.   20

Decay now takes hold of the frame,
breathes despite, motionless – hemmed.
Eyes do not roll, blink no more,
grieving shadows flock the door.
Worldly efforts seem in vain,   25
God's will to prevail in the end.
Hush in the air, palms in fold,
how long will the life hold!

Moments thrive in Vedic chant,
gloom stares at the bedside lamp,   30
that weaves smoke into the vacant sky,
measuring path to heaven, so high.
Gathering eyes take a dolent look,
the distressed in harness never shook.
Hush in the air, palms in fold,   35
at all the life shall any more hold!

The flame darkens, burns still,
at God's mercy or will;
mind and soul on rapt vigil,
clinging to the mortal from looming evil.   40
Hold the flame guarded from gale,
lest the mortal eludes the veiled.

Comes the day of reckoning then,
shadowy hands smother the flame.
Mercy shown to the mortal, that maims,   45
shuts the mind but soul sees no end.
Cremated is the mortal with the mind,
the soul leaps for a refuge, new find;
dry flowers are swept off soon,
mourners recede, expands the moon.   50

Why at all this antithesis then,
blowing wind from vacuum's end!
Euthanasia, if to end the rot,
who is apt to call the shot-
that severs in a wink soul and mind,   55
in a cloak that looks so kind.
Body goes sick -not the rest,
why shear soul for a torn vest!

Should we wish to relieve the soul-
from the malefic trauma of life,   60
try hear the voice of heaven,
who else has the answer precise!

A Foreteller's Web

You,
must it be told,
were born a divine soul,
having brushed past millions doomed to waste,
down the river of fate.
You are precious, though sealed by destiny;
you are shaped - beyond mortal scrutiny.
But take care, there are bends,
there are woes, blinds and trends.
Evil eyes are out to cast,
devil hands are out to dust.
Awake, rise –fight your way out,
seek my advice, if you will-
day in and day out.

Monotony

Monotony- what grills me rather!
Day-night, a grinding wheel;
moon wanes, wiping bright nights,
seasons turn around, years gather.

Dawn descends to sip nectar,   5
fairies sprinkle on grass in the night;
chirping birds fill rhapsody in the air,
not enough to turn me bright.

Day breaks predictably as ever,
strollers stage a walk to rewind;   10
walking alleys are but the same,
floating faces change nearly never.

Stray dogs sniff through the bins
to return soon in vain,
teens scurry for stealthy mates,   15
speed-stars whiz past now and then.

Markets display familiar stuff,
novelty, what is rare to come by;
dishes revisit sooner than later,
turning recipe vapid and bluff.   20

News breaks on media screen -
often wild, often foul politicking;
never ending soap operas linger,
ad blitz sneaks into every other thing.

Songsters bask in remixes,   25
voices doctored to mimic melodies;
ballads and sonnets no more a bind,
stillborn scores pre-empt releases.

Sentiments, not basics, oscillate stocks,
gurus seldom revert to minnows;   30
leaders sham learning through failings,
weathermen heave blame on El Nino.

Often boring is a match of soccer,
fruitless running between the ends;
socials extract a smile or two, and   35
angels pass when silence descends!

Carnivals or festivals are moments of joy,
formats and celebrations remain the same;
deities and shrines have feigned divinity,
who can escape their age old ploy!   40

Upper or Lower Houses or Assembly,
sessions start but soon to adjourn;
democracy hangs in a cliff of debates,
citizens' concerns made a travesty.

Among all that add up to monotony,   45
I could recount but a few;
listless days do tramp down time,
life creeps for fate to brew.

Child's giggle, plants and flowers,
vases, decors, pots and canvas;   50
fort, minaret, war or truce,
cloud, flash, storm, deluge;
birth or demise, shroud or draper,
riddles, shadows, silhouettes and abstracts.

Ah! What else rejuvenates me,   55
are a few but sure to eye;
changing horizon or a poem,
or a wander into the clear night sky.

Dry Petals (Ghazal)

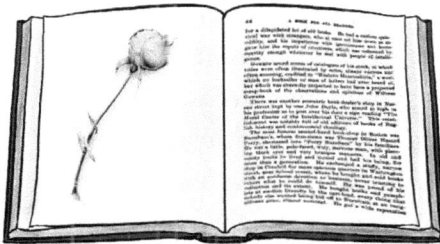

When a song begins with an outro,
when a string snaps mid-rhapsody,
where a river changes course upstream,
when wind moves away from sail
to turn a voyage rudderless in mid sea;   5
so you parted, reasons not known to me.

Ripples that floated on your forehead,
fallen jaw that drifted the face,
void looks you held in blinkless worries,
must have receded behind you, in relief.   10
Must you now be free from all woes!
since, no more shall I be there in you.

Admirers, shall there be around you,
seekers, shall be there to surround you,
queen bee of hive, shall they make of you,   *15*
flowers they pluck, shall ever die for you;
I shall but not be there in your celebrations.

Time drags its feet to move along,
heart slows to starve the capillaries,
breath gasps for air from doldrums,   *20*
hope rots in the marshes of depression;
gone past all innuendos you had, perhaps-
no more am I there in your party.

Someday, if you choose to come back,
someday, if you woo to soothe my woes,   *25*
someday, if you try turn a new leaf;
you may then find dry petals,
reliced between strained pages.

A Tale of an Egg

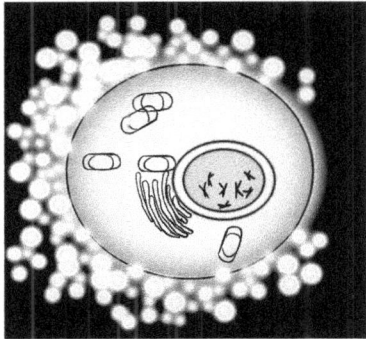

Colony of eggs,
human oocytes in millions
awaiting a chance to fructify,
if God only be on one's side!
Or else, flow inanimate   5
in countless millions,
into the silent sea of fate.
The fortunate finds a mate,
in spring or haste.
Else, get harvested from the deep,   10
and flash-frozen into cryogenic grip -
to wake for a mate sometime soon,
and end the epochal voyage:
who knows – a bane or boon!

Labonyo, at the mid-way   15
of her thirties - a single entity
leads a software team overseas-
a frequent flyer to continents.
Dons a hard protective shell
around her soft, introvert core,   20
she designed over the years
to deflect vagary of proximity
that often comes her way.

Labonyo had frozen her eggs
some years back   25
to retain viability and health.
Thus, liberated she felt -
freed from the pressure of
having to choose
a soulmate in haste.   30

Now, she can take her sweet time,
and not hurry into a relationship
of any kind.
Freed again from hearing
her biological clock ticking,   35
that got louder as she toiled
for a sleep late at night;
or, every time she is airborne -
with her septuagenarian mother
left behind to no one's care,   40
her feelings none to share.

She can now have a child
from the frozen eggs,
stored with much thought and cost.
She has thus saved herself   45
from the events that loom-
of infertility spelling doom,
or advancing grave disability,
or having to go under
consequential treatments,   50
or even career taking precedence
over her soul and body.

As time flows - quiet and relentless,
she senses a change sneaking into her,
that she wouldn't like to share;   55
not even with me – her 'poet of melancholy'!
Here are quiet revelations from her diary:

"My days are no more the same,
ever since the baby-eggs were laid to sleep
in the deep-cool clinical bed.   60
A baby appears every now and then
wading through the haze of my mind:
big black eyes, with moving lips
slipping out some whispers, eyes twitching -
often blurring the screen of my desk-top.   65
Hallo world – hallo world - I grope!

Often I take a detour way back home
or slip out in some pretext,
for a glance of the Clinic
caring for the baby-eggs in sleep;   70
doing so, I get immense peace.

Days turn into months and years,
but time hasn't matured to wake them up;
I only extended the waiting, year after year,
and alibied my hectic job for the holdup.   75

Expectedly, the expiry warning comes about,
eight long years - since I conceived
the baby in my thoughts,
but my search for a soul mate is tiring out!
I can't even share it with   80
the ailing mother in her eighties.
I struggle for days, pondering
whether to let the baby-eggs expire,
Or to donate to someone in need,
that the baby gets a father   85
from a womb that's not mine indeed!

My search for a soul mate
deferred to another day.
My project has since moved overseas,
for a long haul this time.   90

Once again, I'm airborne -
the runway markings, the airport lights
all run amok in pain,
leaving a streak of emptiness in the night sky."

Lonely Orbit

A full moon shines alone
through the melting night,
roves over a consumed earth,
looking for depleted souls
among numb humans - cocooned   5
between high walls and
losing their bright moments
in the opacity of sleep.
The onliest moon ambles
in the wilderness of the sky,   10
leaving the earth unaware.

Back on the trail,
the moon shines again-
waned a speck in weariness,
tracks down   15
through a film of dust,
calmed on a window pane,
a pair of blinkless eyes
denied sleep
in pains of solitude;   20
the moon finds a solace
in her lonesome orbit.

Apartheid

Reared in isolation,
set apart by land and sea;
minds stray yet light-years afar,
abound with barriers that be.

Genetic prints they bear,   5
of heat and dust - very own;
looks differ but skin-deep,
blood, sweat or tears - intone.

One did outpace the other,
the way they worked their mind;   10
ploughed their way through the ages,
with tact, power and grind.

Colonial 'Apartness' born of greed,
conquered through cruelty extreme;
homo sapiens sorted by colour of skin,   15
ripped through their homes serene.

White nursed but ailing white,
hate removed church from church;
natives carried passes on person,
lest they trespass the land of birth.   20

Racism returned with face anew,
time mellowed to change its stance;
evil spirits stalked ghettos and streets,
groups took reins, nations beat a retreat.

Time though turns a full circle now,   25
hate simmers still in mind so deep;
kindled across clans and kin,
if legacy to end, who can vow!

Justice or requital–a work in process,
led by crusaders, leaders and minds;   30
Gandhi, King, Tutu or Mandela -
all came from the oppressed kinds.

Where've the tyrants gone hiding,
the discerning world is sick;
doling out at global venues,   35
not enough to calm the prey of pique.

Malaise deeper than one thinks,
among clans and homes of my land;
dark skin tagged low in circles,
spurned in pomp, blitz and brand.   40

Tell me!
Why whiten a face in makeover,
what shame you need to hide!
what if a show man's skin is dark,
why blink at the dark in colour divide.   45
why a horse be called dark,
if the win is a surprise!

Doesn't it rain when clouds hang dark!
Aren't berries ripe as they turn dark!
To soothe our eyes we cover it dark,   50
time too shared between light and dark.

It's a pity,
dusky lasses are led into white dreams,
let profit zoom for fairness creams!

The Exodus

The escape

The sky hung overcast,
the air heavy in eerie silence,
the danger stared imminent,
with no God or saviour around,
and the carnage caught up soon.   5
They all ran amok,
away or into the ferocity,
had no moments for shock or the sick,
or for the old or those not around;
the hearth, the pets and the orchard -   10
soon, they all fell behind.

They skirted the onslaught in passage,
many though felled by thirst and hunger,
by maladies and plunder;
made their way through woods and dunes,   15
human streams turned a river soon -
across hostile lands and fugitives.

Lost many faces on the way,
winning many hearts, nonetheless;
a few reached the gateway of hope,   20
to embark upon an audacious quest
for the coveted haven!
The ordeal started then,
in blood and flesh.

* * *

The voyage

A pack of icy faces,   25
jutting eyes, mirroring imminent death;
women clinging children to the breast,
men holding grit to the last.
A patch of aloof starry sky above,
high waves effacing dark skyline below,   30
furious hungry sea out to swallow
everything that rode its waves.
The laden boat
in ceaseless roll and pitch,
now succumbs fading cries amidst,   35
leaving no trace
of the intrepid spirit that sailed,
on a voyage of hope and survival.
The sharks now gather for more feeds,
human epic in thousands   40
lost thus in watery grave-
into gloom so deep.

* * *

73

The Fences

Human floats fished out of sea, and
those survived land misery;
fleeing poverty, strife, war or persecution,   45
they swelled into sparkles on the move.

Dazed, thirsty and hungry,
near ones - lost, waylaid.
Children unescorted, isolated -
they are but uprooted vines,   50
creeping for a bed of earth.

Migrants and refugees - their new tags,
crammed into trucks or ships,
hot, airless, dark carriages
for loopy, unspecified trips.   55
Perilous crossing in traffickers' boats,
belongings strewn across beaches;
human tsunami now swamps Europe,
unwanted they are, amidst heartfelt reaches.

Screaming babies at the razor-wire fence,   60
deported those not of safe origins.
Attempts to hold back migration floodgate,
anti-immigrant backlashes quick to surface.
Chance entrants languish in makeshift camps,
brutal winter numbs ill-fed bones;   65
moral and legal pathways shunned,
populist media take warring stance.

Refugee right turns empty noise,
relocation plan or Dublin voice;
fortress Europe is divided within,   70
building borders- not harmonise asylum.
Globalisation of hatred makes northward trip,
it's a death of civilisation, a coma the least.

* * *

Trampled Garden

They trampled your sovereign garden
of pedigreed grass and flowers,   75
you nurtured with pride and care,
in centuries of renaissance and war.
Outlandish weeds and shrubs,
creeping into your idyllic pasture,
out to strangle turf and hedges   80
you grew with sweat and love.

The ethnic waves of the 'Hinder Sea'
breaking on your serene shore, bring-
laden boats of woes and dreams,
and floating debris of lifeless siblings.   85

The cloud of doom that gathered
over their hallowed land in curse,
now sails into your blissful sky
to soon descend in rain ominous.
Swirling storm from distant dunes   90
now mingle with your Alpine wind;
spray hot sands of puzzle and angst
on crevices of your Gothic wings.
The blue blood running in your veins
being threatened with ignoble flow,   95
from people you play host now,
but demeaned and despised then.

Appears, as though the vicious time
has chosen to turn full circle now,
to owe the man apology for breaches   100
committed in your hey days and prime.
Human disasters, history gone through,
the modern world isn't immune either;
justice is blindfold, so are inventions,
abegging goes our wisdom to dither.   105

* * *

Disquiet

Alarming! Where the globe is leading to,
agents of doom in guise to destroy you;
millions destitute out to feel the wrath
of weak link of bonding that alienates you.

Loosely held on a shaky pedestal,   110
human progress at a juncture critical;
reprisal and vengeance to assume the reins,
lands and races - livid, inimical.

Weapons of mass killing soon to follow,
as Fedayeen strikes fail to wallow.   115
No place or person has immunity of life,
new designs excel in ingenuity and style;
frontiers cave in to districts and towns,
sovereignty, a misnomer – governments frown.

Clotted Poem

I hear: bone chilling chorus of a billion cries,
surging across landscapes the world over;
twenty first century mirroring medieval age,
even as triumphant man enters mesmeric space.

I discern : vying religions, dogged followers,   5
bigots, sects, groups and preachers
on a remorseless killing spree;
not to spare women and children,
not even heritage shrines;
fleeing millions stashed or slashed   10
erasing race with gelatine sticks,
only to shore up patented rights
of their inherited god
they would never face.

I rue : the world, down and out,   15
who knows count of their lot!
Stricken with hunger, abuse and virus,
rickety children disowned – shuddered
by kin and onlookers alike;
others bring pittance, with fanfare.   20

I shiver: at melting glaciers -
shifting earth's gravity,
tilting its axis,
slowing rotation time down,
to effects unknown.   25

I shudder: sinking cities and tossing hearths,
in tornado, cyclone and surge;
emission fast choking city-lungs,
blissfully actions sought out far flung.
Broking satraps of haves and nots,   30
raise storm in forums' tea pots-
across tables of felled mahogany and teak;
tigers are reared to guard forests,
poachers thrive in woods so deep.

I vex : mafia and warlords -   35
spreading roots far into systems;
states and armies overwhelmed,
or often seen conniving;
drugs and narcotics build their nest,
weave into human zest.   40

I deplore : elites parading in Davos or Rio,
thumping chests over own exploits;
lucky few earn in dignity,
many more toil in devils' firms,
and the rest live in abject poverty.   45

I fret : fleeing migrants -
sail for mystic shores of fortune and peace;
Across choppy Seas; while, nations squabble
to wash their hands,
we draw a rainbow of 'one world'.   50

I palpitate : nations flexing nukes in hypocrisy,
forgotten are Hiroshima and Nagasaki;
stockpile enough to kill all over,
rigged ballots create fake democracy.
School girls scooped, remain untracked,   55
when shameless republics plead infirmity;
world thus turn into cubicles of inverses,
euphoric leaders fumble for their faculty.

I seethe : With anger at state sponsored crime,
breaches, U-turns, proliferation shine;   60
new wave vanguards duck under oath,
divide effaced between citizen and sleuth.

I Ruminate : TRP and paid news arming media,
free and dissenting voice they thwart;
history patented, truth buried in time,   65
colour of skin stokes, societies torn apart.
Space junks, nuclear wastes and non-recyclables,
widen the noose, as we grope and squabble in dark.
Where do I end up with such narrations!
Poems can't be verses of ruinations.   70

My poem clots into a prose,
mind loses flux and flow:
in this din of holocaust
selfie of the time to never glow.

Eternal Debt

Tell me mom, for once
how much you love me!
Weigh up for once mom
how much I owe thee!

I looked up and chanced a glance   5
at saline crystals in her eyes;
behind stood the Sun in smile,
as answers in me came to rise.

Juvenile as I am in many ways,
to wrap up with thanks for mom;   10
for, my debt that never ceases,
more I strive, more it increases.

The Sun since travelled distances,
many times over, many times;
I grew in her web of love –   15
selfless, cool, silent, divine!

My world has now no time to spare,
fond images come and go;
but the like of a mother is none,
her aura shines, my path to glow.   20

The Imposters

love thy love live,
emotions live as long;
lest it litters lives,
turning into a live-evil.

piece thine aim trussed together,   5
not to retail peace for gain;
moments left are so very scarce,
use before thou see them slain.

coarse speech ruffles placid mind,
that takes longer to get on course;   10
knot that loses its way en route,
may not listen to crying hoarse.

one wins aye over two
to tow the lot toeing it;
teacher taught tots through hymns,   15
keeping eyes shut all the time.

bees gather honey in the hive,
emptying flowers of sweet nectar;
child sucks mother's milk,
be strong to grow bigger.   20

should thou be drawing
a rightful share
of nature's bounty spread for thee,
must thou save to draw first
a portrait of harmony in lieu;   25
for, once broken the fine line,
no more shall it break
into blissful symphony anew.

kindness rests aloft virtues,
where the rest is placed before self;   30
when soul, the sole churner of will
gets tired of idle time,
high altar encased in us
shall alter the course in narrow mind;
that alone would lead us to route   35
to the root of life divine.

how do they design letters
to cut a long short,
rest assured dear readers
to make it quicker than trot.   40
read or get rid of it,
own or leave it rather,
option lies but with thee
as words belie one another.

characters aren't all that mine,   45
but mined from the mind in play;
one preys on the other's kinship,
makes despite, the sense thy pray.

Statues Come Alive

Poets, Philosophers, Painters and Writers,
Patriots, Performers, Inventors and Liberators,
Reformers, Saints, Gladiators and Dictators,
Beauties, Royalties, Mermaids and Dinosaurs:
stoic or assertive winners of plinths,   5
adorning street junctions, parks,
memorials and monuments -
with their towery statues,
of marble, granite or bronze-
to ram in longevity.   10
Owing posterity and devout zealots-
had this way to bow and idolise
their deeds, exploits and charms.
Wash and bouquets offered to some,
to ritualise commemorations,   15
others given a pass in the milieu.

Numb and motionless,
with no vocal cord grafted,
mutely they watch hurried time
pass by relentlessly.   20
No let up in their assigned task
of a passive curator of history,
or of servicing their debt of fame -
a fait accompli.
Time ages into years   25
and years into decades and millennium.
Some find reprieve
when devalued and demolished,
others wear off from wind, heat and rain-
in a natural death.   30

In their hay days on plinth,
how did they tick their time
or beat off quarantine,
I wonder!
Did anyone hear their unguarded whispers,   35
I wonder!
What thoughts had flicked their frozen minds,
I wonder!

If ever, they descended from their plinths
on a desolate street,   40
in a foggy wintry night,
holding each other's hands,
exchanging reminiscences of their time,
or, a veiled Rebecca being moved
from the glitters seen   45
in the eyes of a lovelorn poet,
or, a dictator seeking saint's pardon
for presiding onslaught,
or, a dinosaur revealing true stories
of the catastrophe,   50
or, the king turning emotional
at the homeless in rags
coping the bite of winter,
or, the inventor's penitence
over discovery of gun powder.   55
Perhaps, they filled the night air
with animated conclave
on aborted tales of history.
With dawn descending in soft-foot
they retired to their plinths,   60
carrying memories of the night before.

Day rolls over to another night,
that sees brisk activities on streets;
so they spend a sleepless time,
in thought of missing midnight summit.   65
Then, news has gone around-
the patriot to be razed the next day,
at the behest of the new regime.
Tremor shakes their plinths in anger,
dew drops roll down their cheeks   70
through the apocalyptic night;
they freeze to statues, once more-
never to come alive.

Shiver

A ripple runs through me softly,
a lace of raga
from the strings of a distant sitar
churning my soul, of late
in an inexplicable feeling,   5
or is it the onset of an early winter,
or a southern wind
sailing moisture from the bay,
or is this the shiver
a sky droplet induces on a leaf!   10

Days tread often soft foot,
carrying resonance along, unheard;
longing goes often wayward,
looking for a new pasture;
life but often relents over   15
flow that was slated to be;
cosmic ions storm the wishes,
who knows what it turns to be!

Resolute is the time
in beat and fairness,   20
stubborn pieces
too are carried along,
What seems a block
on its course today,
may pave the way   25
to a spring before long.

Life and Death

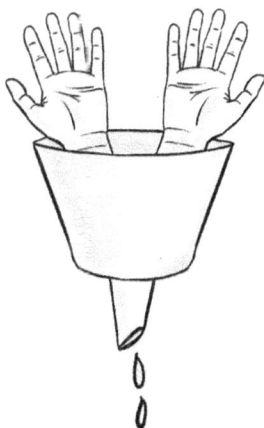

Then he was a chip
of the living block
in blood and flesh,
indulging, dynamic, often balky.

Shared the air to breathe,   5
of the sun drew in the heat,
roamed the earth at will to bind,
soaked up season that fell behind,
hailed by names, one or two,
clubbed with the clan he grew -   10
for bond and identity;
took liberty to fall apart
or stayed entwined at will of heart;
lived moments of love or hate,
when mind and body were in spate.   15
Grew in his own world,
within a world of dissenting voice;
often cocooned himself
in a shell of unforced choice;
led life in rituals and blind belief,   20
or with the beacon glow inside.
Left a mark of his own, low or high,
for posterity to treasure or despise.
Stories, so dearly he engraved on sand -
that shuffled to throw his life into relief.   25

Now he is laid on a pyre or in a box,
ending all jibes and talks.
Eyes are wet all around,
few probing minds too abound.
End came slow or fast,   30
now was he there on feet,
now on a journey, to never meet.

Once an imposing height,
turned a cadaver of water, protein,
collagen and amino acid.   35
Soon to perish, into clay and dust
or through an alkaline hydrolysis,
into a sterile brown effluent -
to recycle into strange matters,
to recede into the mists of the past.   40

Stillness of Motion

Feet cross-legged, with knees folded,
placed on opposite thighs,
toes pointed upward,
knees drawn close together,
groin pressed towards the floor,   5
spine straight,
hands rested on knees, palms upward
creating a circle
with each index finger and thumb,
other fingers extended;   10
face softened, gaze to "third eye"
body relaxed, kept in controlled breath,
mind sunk in deep stillness.

I return thus
to Padmasana – the meditative Yoga   15
from a daylong roundup of
the metropolis, for a living;
I take the feel of the Earth below,
that seeps up to lift the mind
and the spirit.   20

The quiescence of the 'Asana'
now blends with a motion
never felt before!
I'm a cosmic being -
inseparable from   25
the large scheme of things,
not entitled to stillness;
I'm on a ride,
trying to catch the speed of light.
I rotate, I revolve, and I slide   30
at a god sent speed,
carrying microbes and granules along,
across endless galaxies -
towards the Great Attractor.
Such is the speed of my stillness!   35
I slide a thousand kilometers a second -
whether I like it or not,
believe it or not!

Woman

Have you ever loved a woman -
even in thoughts and dreams?
Of any shape, color or creed,
rude, reticent or romantic.
Speaks from her throat, teeth or lips,   5
or from her subtle dreamy eyes envied.
Who is a parched stream,
or a cascading brook in flow,
or whose warmth comes from
a steamy sulphur spring -   10
to enliven life to glow,
or an empty heart-
loath to echo
an emotional spurt.

Or you loved a passing shower,   15
a bed of season flower,
an invading tsunami in rage -
carrying all you had in its wave,
a placid mountain -
erupting avalanche,   20
to growl and roll for days,
thorny cactus of a dry stretch -
deflecting your persona and grace!

Or an iceberg in poles -
melting for years of   25
agony and neglect abysmal,
or serving a split heart in you
with all her faithful soul -
drowsing her oppressed needs
with pittance reaching as a dole.   30

From the highway, far away
where sun-baked fields give way,
a non-descript village unfolds
from sleepy orchard and coppices;
twilight sets in layers of gloom,   35
wakes up the Hesperus in the west.
A little away, across a clay-top yard,
a woman with an oil-lamp on her palm
walks up to her deity of heart-
a sapling of Tulsi on a pedestal;   40
raises her heart in shriek ululation,
amidst sounding of conch shell
and spiraling aromatic smoke
of sacrificial joss sticks held aloft.
She bows before the sacred Tulsi -   45
offering her submerged soul,
praying for the return of her man
from the shadows, he was lost.

www.ingramcontent.com/pod-product-compliance
Lightning Source LLC
LaVergne TN
LVHW041323080426
835513LV00008B/573